THE FIRST BOOK OF MEN:
INSTRUCTIONS OF SHURUPPAK

Abu Salabikh
Amber Snow

© 20th Century Publishing 2022

ISBN 9798416095130

Contents

Preface 1

How to Read the Text 3

Instructions of Shuruppak 5

Instructions of Shuruppak: Commentary 15

Preface

In the Instructions of Shuruppak, dating to about 4,600 years ago, a Sumerian king gave his son a series of proverbs to guide him in his conduct. Written on clay tablets, the ancient writings are some of the world's earliest surviving literary works in existence. Several scholars have connected the Shuruppak Instructions to the Ten Commandments and other biblical proverbs.

Shuruppak's Instructions might be seen as an early example of "wisdom literature", a kind of ancient Near Eastern literature. It is a collection of wisdom from sage and intelligent men and women on the subject of God and morality. Despite the fact that this genre makes use of oral storytelling skills, it has mostly been spread via print media.

The ruler of Shuruppak, the final Sumerian monarch to govern before the Great Flood, is credited for writing the Instructions of Shuruppak. The Sumerian King Lists include the name of this king's father, Ubara-Tutu, who is claimed to have lived 18,500 years before the Great Flood ravaged Mesopotamia. To his son, Ziusudra, the king of Shuruppak gives guidance in the Instructions of Shuruppak. For his role in the Epic of Gilgamesh, Ziusudra (known in the Akkadian text as Utnapishtin) is possibly the most famous figure. When this king was born, his name meant "obtain long life", which is related to the fact that, according to the archives, he supposedly ruled for 36,000 years. Ziusudra, rather than Shuruppak, is listed as the final king before the flood in one version of the Sumerian King List.

The words "In those days, in those far-flung days, in those nights, in those far-flung nights, in those years, in those far-flung years" appear at the beginning of one version of the Instructions of Shuruppak, indicating that the events that follow occurred in the distant past, when "Shuruppak, the wise one who knew how to speak in elaborate words, lived in the Land;".

Shuruppak advises against stealing and having sex with married women in the first of three sections of the book. As much as these guidelines encourage the reader to live an ethical life, there is also a practical component to them. After each piece of advice, the author of the book explains why he gave it. When it comes to theft and adultery, it's important to keep in mind that the consequences of both are dire.

In the second section, there is a tendency to deliver positive directions more often. In the third section, both positive and negative forms are provided in about equal measure.

How to Read the Text

Beside the translation, we provide a transliteration of the original cuneiform system of writing. Some parts of the original tablets are damaged or difficult to read. Therefore this has given rise to different transliterations. When the cuneiform symbol is hardly visible we include an "X" into the transliteration to mean damaged symbol. When there are broken parts of the clay tablets or missing segments, we use three dots "..." to indicate the absence of symbols.

The text is preceded by numbers that refer to the line in the original tablets. Our translation is identified by the first part of the text, in bold. The transliteration follows the translation and is followed by some explanation on the translation provided, including translations of some symbols that might help the reader to understand why we have translated the text in certain ways. Some ambiguity exists in some parts, which is indicated by a question mark "(?)". We do not provide a word-by-word translation, as this requires explaining the complex Sumerian grammar. However, the many words translated should be sufficient to help the reader grasp the meaning of the sentence and provide their own interpretation of the text.

A few words are required to explain the somewhat strange look of transliteration to the unfamiliar reader. Sumerian nouns may take on many forms at the same time. It is a trait that they share with both the adjectives, the nouns and the verbs in the sentence. The reduplication of a noun entails the complete repeating of the noun's stem. The traditional way to spell a term that has been duplicated is to write it twice. Reduplication is a complex grammar construct that could imply many different meanings. Verbs that use reduplication somewhat imply a repetition of the action described. For example, the term *hal* can be translated to say "to stream, run (a river); divide; drain a reservoir". If used with the meaning of dividing, then *hal* can be translated in a sentence as "I divided", whereas the reduplication form *hal-hal* would become "I was (repeatedly) dividing (it)". Partial reduplication can also be used to make a distinction between past and present. For example, hal "I divided it", hal-ha "(it) divides".

Reduplication can intensify an adjective. For example, a big city is uru-gal, and a really big city is uru-gal-gal. For nouns, it can be used to transform the singular into plural, e.g., uru (city), uru-uru (cities) and is believed to signify totality. For example, kur-kur means "all foreign lands".

It is also important to be aware that the cuneiform system often uses many marks to represent the same sound. During transliteration, it is critical to know the precise signs that were used by the scribe. This is why, when transliterating, historians employ numerals and accents to indicate which is which. The numbers may sometimes go rather large, see for example *ge26*. These numbers and accents are critical because symbols with the same pronunciation might have a variety of meanings.

We have provided the translation of the first seventy lines of transliterated text with a dictionary, associating words with meaning. In some cases, we have given the reasoning behind a certain choice for the translation. We believe this extra material can help the reader to understand in more depth the intricacies of the cuneiform text.

Instructions of Shuruppak

In those days, in those far-flung days, in those nights, in those far-flung nights, in those years, in those far-flung years, at that time, Shuruppak, the wise one who knew how to speak in elaborate words, lived in the Land; Shuruppak, the wise one who knew how to speak in elaborate words, lived in the Land. Shuruppak instructed his son; Shuruppak, the son of Ubara-Tutu, instructed his son Zi-ud-sura: My son, allow me to teach you: pay attention! Allow me to utter a word to you, Zi-ud-sura: you should pay attention! Take care not to disregard my directions! Please do not violate the words I utter! The old man's teachings are priceless; you should follow them!

You should avoid purchasing a braying donkey; it will split (?) your midriff (?).
You should not situate a field next to a road; You should not plough a field along a path; You should avoid digging a well in your field; others will damage it. You should avoid building adjacent to a public plaza since it is always crowded (?)

You should not vouch for someone because that person will have influence over you, and you should not vouch for yourself (that man will despise (?) you).

You should not examine (?) a man because the flood (?) will return it to you (?)

You should not linger around a conflict; you should not allow the quarrel to turn you into a witness. You should not allow (?) yourself to get embroiled in a disagreement. You should avoid inciting a conflict;............... the palace's gate...... Take a step back from a conflict,....... you should not take (?) another route.

You should not steal anything; you should abstain from...... You should avoid breaking into a home and wishing for the money box (?). A thief is a lion, but once caught, he becomes a slave. My son, you should abstain from robbery and avoid self-injury with an axe.

You should avoid appointing a young guy as best man. You should refrain from...... on your own. You should use caution while dealing with a married young woman: the defamation might be severe. My son, you must not sit alone in a room with a married lady.

You should avoid starting a fight and humiliating yourself. You must not tell lies;...You should not boast; otherwise, your claims will be dismissed. You should avoid prolonged deliberation (?); you cannot stand...stares.

You should avoid sharing stolen food with others. You should avoid immersing your hand (?) in blood. After you have distributed the bones, you will be required to repair the ox and the sheep.

You should avoid speaking badly; this will eventually set you up for failure.

You should not disperse your flock to unfamiliar pastures. You should never employ someone else's ox for an unclear... A secure...... entails a secure trip.

You should avoid traveling at night since it may conceal both good and evil.

You should avoid purchasing an onager, since it only lasts (?) until the end of the day.

You should abstain from having sexual relations with your slave girl; she will eat you up (?).

Do not curse vehemently: it will come back to haunt you.

You should avoid drawing up water that is beyond your grasp. This will make you weak.

You should avoid driving a debtor away, since he will become resentful of you.

You should avoid establishing a house with an arrogant guy because he would treat you like a slave girl. You will be unable to enter any human habitation without being accosted: "There you have it! There you have it!"

You should not remove the reed fence from the garden; "Replenish it! Replenish it! "They will tell you.

You should not feed a stranger (?) or resolve (?) a fight.

My son, you should abstain from using violence (?);... You should abstain from raping someone's daughter; the courtyard will find out.

You should not attempt to drive away a strong guy; you should not attempt to demolish the outer wall. You should never push a young guy away; you should never turn him against the city. The slanderer's eyes are always as nimble as a spindle. You should never stay in his presence; you should not allow his intentions (?) to have an influence (?) on you.

You should not brag like a deceptive guy in beer halls : (At that point, your statements will be taken seriously.)

After becoming an adult, you should refrain from leaping (?) with your hand. The warrior is unique; he is the only one who is equal to many; Utu is unique; he is the only one who is equal to many. Always put your life on the side of the warrior; always put your life on the side of Utu.

Shuruppak instructed his son on these matters. Shuruppak, the son of Ubara-Tutu, instructed his son Zi-ud-sura in these matters. Shuruppak instructed his son a second time. Shuruppak, the son of Ubara-Tutu, instructed his son Zi-ud-sura as follows: My son, allow me to offer you some instructions. You should pay attention! Allow me to utter a word to you, Zi-ud-sura: you should pay attention! Take care not to disregard my directions! Please do not violate the words I utter! (An elderly man's instructions are priceless; you should follow them!)

The lips of a beer drinker...... My little one......The lips of a beer drinker...... Ninkasi......

Your own guy will not compensate (?) you. Reed beds are......; they may conceal (?) defamation.

The palace is like a vast river; what pours in is never enough to fill it, and what flows out is unstoppable.

When it comes to another person's bread, it's simple to say, "I'll give it to you," but the moment of real offering might be as far as the sky. If you pursue the guy who said "I will give it to you," he would respond, "I am unable to offer it to you since the bread has just been consumed."

Property is something to be extended (?); yet, nothing compares to my little children.

The creative mouth speaks words; the harsh mouth delivers court records; and the sweet mouth harvests delicious plants.

The garrulous delivers a full sack of bread; the arrogant brings an empty bag and can only fill his empty mouth with bragging.

Anyone who works with leather will ultimately (?) have to work with his or her own leather.

The powerful can elude (?) anyone's grasp.

The idiot is deprived of something. The idiot loses something while he sleeps. "Do not shackle me!" he cries; "Let me live!" he cries.

The imprudent determines fortunes; the shameless heaps (?) things into the lap of another: "I am such that I deserve respect." Fate has a way of seizing (?) a weak lady.

If you employ a worker, he or she will share the bread bag with you; he or she will eat from the bag alongside you and will complete the bag with you. Then he will stop working for you and, claiming, "I must earn a living," he will service in the palace.

You call your son to your home, and you call your daughter to her women's quarters. When you consume beer, you should refrain from passing judgment.
You should not be excessively concerned with what exits the home.

Although heaven is the farthest away and earth the most valuable, it is via heaven that you increase your possessions and all distant nations breathe.

At harvest season, the most valuable period of the year, gather like a slave girl and eat like a queen; my son, this is how it should be; to collect like a slave girl and eat like a queen is how it should be.

Whoever insults has the potential to injure just the flesh; hungry eyes (?) on the other hand, have the potential to murder.

The liar, yelling, rips his clothes to shreds. Insults serve as (?) counsel to the wicked. Arrogance is like an abscess: a stomach-turning weed.

My prayers bring many blessings. Prayer is like a calm stream that soothes the heart. Only (?) insults and dumb speech get the Land's attention.

Shuruppak instructed his son on these matters. Shuruppak, the son of Ubara-Tutu, instructed his son Zi-ud-sura in these matters.

Shuruppak instructed his kid a third time. Shuruppak, the son of Ubara-Tutu, instructed his son Zi-ud-sura as follows: My son, allow me to offer you some instructions. You should pay attention! Allow me to utter a word to you, Zi-ud-sura: you should pay attention! Take care not to disregard my directions! Please do not violate the words I utter! (An elderly man's teachings are priceless; you should follow them!)

You should not retaliate against a farmer's son: he built (?) your embankments and ditches.

You should never buy a prostitute because she has a biting tongue. You should not purchase a house-born slave: he is a stomach-turning weed. You should never purchase a free guy; he will always lean against the wall. You should never purchase a palace slave girl: she will always be second-rate (?). You should rather bring a foreign slave down from the highlands or bring someone from a region where he is an alien. My son, he will pour water for you where the sun rises and will go ahead of you. He is not a member of any family, and so has no desire to visit his family; he is also not a member of any city, and thus has no desire to visit his city. (He is not permitted to knock on the door of......, he is not permitted to enter......) He will not be arrogant towards you. He will not be arrogant towards you.

You should not go alone eastward, my son. Your friend should refrain from...

A name superimposed over another......; you should not build a mountain on top of another.

Fate is like a wet bank; it is capable of making a single error.

The oldest brother is, in fact, similar to a father; the elder sister is, in fact, similar to a mother. Therefore, you should listen to your older brother and be as submissive to your elder sister as if she were your mother.

You should not work only with your eyes; only using your tongue won't help you earn more money. The careless one destroys (?) his family.

The necessity for food compels some people to climb the mountains; it also compels traitors and outsiders to descend, as the need for food compels other people to descend.

A tiny city gifts (?) a calf to its monarch; a large city digs (?) a home plot (?).

...... is equipped to the hilt. The poor guy infects the affluent man with a variety of diseases. The married guy is well-equipped; the single man must make his bed in a haystack (?). Whoever intends to demolish a home will do so; whoever wishes to elevate it will do so.

You can cross the river by gripping the neck of a massive ox. By following (?) the strong men of your city, my son, you will undoubtedly climb (?).

When you bring a slave girl from the hills into your home, she carries with her both good and bad. The ability to do good is in the hands; the ability to do evil is in the heart. The heart will not abandon the good; nevertheless, it will not abandon the wicked either. As if the heart were a body of water, it does not forsake the good. Evil is a warehouse...

May the evil-boat doer's drown in the river! May his water-skin crack in the sands of the desert!

A loving heart helps to sustain a family; a cruel heart helps to destroy a family.

Having authority, possessing property, and being firm are princely divine abilities. You should submit to those who are respected; you should be modest in the presence of those who are strong. You will then survive (?) against the wicked, my son.

You should avoid marrying at a festival. Her interior is illusory (?), as is her exterior. Her silver is borrowed, as is her lapis lazuli (the jewellery on her is borrowed, the jewellery on her is borrowed). Her outfit is borrowed, as is the linen robe she is wearing. Nothing (?) compares to...

You should avoid purchasing a...... bull. You should avoid purchasing a dangerous bull;...... a gap (?) in the cattle pen... One selects (?) a trustworthy lady to run a well-run family.

You should not purchase a donkey during the harvest season. A donkey that consumes...... will be associated with another donkey.

Although a violent donkey hangs its neck, a vicious man, my son,......

A woman who owns property devastates the residence. An inebriated person will drown the harvest.

A female burglar (?) flies inside homes like a fly. On the street, a she-donkey...... On the street, a sow breastfeeds its young. A lady who has poked herself starts to sob and clutches the spindle that punctured (?) her. She enters every home; she glances down every street...... she is always yelling, "Get out!" She scans the area (?) from every parapet. She pants (?) in the presence of a fight.

Marry (?)...... whose heart vehemently despises (?). My son,... ...A heart brimming with delight...

Nothing is worth valuing, but life should be pleasant. You should not serve your possessions; your possessions should serve you. My son,...

You should not... grain; it contains several...

You should never harm an ewe; otherwise, she will have a daughter. You should not place a lump of soil in the money chest (?), since this will result in the birth of a boy.

You should not kidnap your wife; you should refrain from making her weep (?). The location of the wife's abduction...

"Allow us to run in circles (?) while exclaiming, "Oh, my foot!" and "Oh, my neck!" Let us make the powerful bow in unison (?)!"

You should not murder a... since he is a kid produced by... You should not murder him in the manner of...; you should not tie him.

The wet-nurses in the women's quarters decide their lord's destiny.

You should avoid speaking arrogantly to your mother; doing so breeds contempt for you. You should never doubt your mother's or personal god's statements. The mother, like Utu, births the man; the father, like a deity, enlightens him (?). The parent is like to a god: his words are trustworthy. The father's instructions should be followed.

Without suburbs, a city would also lack a central business district.

My son's land, whether wet or dry, is a source of money.

It seems incomprehensible (?) that anything could be lost in perpetuity.

Getting lost is unpleasant for a dog, but dreadful for a man. On the strange path along the mountains' edge, the gods of the mountains are man-eaters. They do not construct homes in the same way that men do; they do not construct towns in the same way that men do.

For the shepherd, he ceased looking and returning the sheep. According to the farmer (?), he stopped plowing the land.

This gift of words has a calming effect on the mind......; as it enters the palace, it has a calming effect on the mind...... The talent of several words..

This is the lesson delivered by Shuruppak, Ubara-son. Praise be to the woman who finished the large tablets, the maiden Nisaba, who instructed Shuruppak, the son of Ubara-Tutu!

Instructions of Shuruppak: Commentary

> 1–13: In those days, in those distant days, in those nights, in those far away nights, in those years, in those far away years, Shuruppak, the wise one who understood how to talk in complicated terms, lived in the Land. Shuruppak taught his son; Shuruppak, the son of Ubara-Tutu, told his son Ziudsura. Allow me to teach you something, my son: pay attention! Allow me to address you directly, Ziudsura: you should give consideration! Be sure not to disobey my commands! Gratefully refrain from violating the words I speak! The elderly man's lessons are invaluable; you should pay attention to them!

Transliterated cuneiform text
1. u4 re-a u4 su3-ra2 re-a
2. ge6 re-a ge6 ba9-ra2 re-a
3. mu re-a mu su3-ra2 re-a
4. u4-ba gestug2 tuku inim galam inim zu-a kalam-ma ti-la-a
5. shuruppakki gesztu2 tuku inim galam inim zu-a kalam-ma ti-la-a
6. shuruppakki-e dumu-ni-ra na na-mu-un-de5-de5
7. shuruppakki dumu ubara-tu-tu-ke4
8. zi-u4-su3-ra2 dumu-ni-ra na na-mu-un-de5-de5
9. dumu-gu10 na ga-de5 na-de5-mu he2-dab5
10. zi-u4-su3-ra2 inim ga-ra-ab-du11 gizzal he2-em-szi-ak
11. na-de5-ga-mu szu nam-bi2-bar-re
12. inim du11-ga-mu na-ab-ta-bal-e-de3
13. na-de5 ab-ba nig2 kal-la-am3 gu2-zu he2-em-szi-gal2

1. u4 re-a "in those days" commonly refers to ancient/primeval times; su3 meaning distant, remote; su3-ra2 distant days.
2. ge6: to be black/night. ge6 re-a: in those nights; ba9-ra2: far

away; ge6 ba9-ra2: in those far away nights.

3. mu: year; mu re-a: in those years; mu su3-ra2 re-a: in those far away years.

4. u4-ba: in those days; gestug2: wise; tuku: to have; inim: word; galam: to understand/be skillful; zu-a: to know; kalam-ma: the Land; ti-la-a: to live. So this can be translated as: "the wise man that was skillful with words, lived in the Land";

5. shuruppakki: Shuruppak; line 5 is a repetition of line 4, with reference so Shuruppak;

6. dumu: son; ni: myself; ni-ra: of myslef; dumu-ni-ra: his son (son of myself with reference to Shuruppak); na: advice; na-mu-un-de5-de5: to collect; The line can be translated as "Shuruppak instructed or taught or gave advice to his son";

7. ubara-tu-tu-ke4: Ubara-Tutu; so "Shuruppak, the son of Ubara-Tutu";

8. zi-u4-su3-ra2: Ziudsura, king of Shuruppak. He is credited as the last king of Sumer prior to the Great Flood. In Akkadian he is know as Utnapishtim (e.g, in the Epic of Gilgamesh);

9. dumu-gu10: kid/son; he2-dab5: to seize. So Shuruppak is instructing his son, Ziudsura;

10. ga-ra-ab-du11: will teach/tell you; gizzal: hearing; he2: be he; em: to be; ak: to do; szi: fill;

11. szu: hand; bar: to set aside; nam: it is a prefix used to form abstract or collective nouns;

12. bal: to turn;

13. ab-ba: father; nig2: thing; kal: to be rare.

> 14: You should avoid purchasing a young donkey; it will split (?) your midriff (?).

Transliterated cuneiform text
14. dur3ur3 gu3 di na-ab-sa10-sa10 murub4-zu sza-ra-ab-si-il

14. dur3ur3: young donkey; gu3: voice; di: right decision; murub4: middle; si-il: to split.

> 15–18: You should not place a field alongside a road; You should not plow a field beside a route; You should avoid digging a well within your field: others will damage it for you. You should avoid building adjacent to a public plaza since it is always crowded (?)

Transliterated cuneiform text
15. gana2 kaskal-la nam-bi2-ib2-ga2-ga2 nam-silig gu2-ga2-am3
16. a-sag2 ka-gir3-ka nam-ba-e-ur11-ru zi bulug-ga-am3
17. gana2-zu-am3 pu2 na-an-ni-dun-e-en ug3-e sza-ri-ib-hul-hul
18. e2 sila dagal nam-bi2-ib-la2-e kesz2-da gal2-la-am3

15. gana2: field; kaskal: road; gar: to place; nam-silig: force; gu2-ga2-am3: *unknown meaning*;
16. a-sag2: field; ka-giri3: path; ur11-ru: to plow; bulug: boundary;
17. zu: to know; pu2: well; dun: to dig; hul: to destroy;
18. sila: public plaza; dagal: copious; la2: abundant.

> 19–20: You should not vouch for anybody: that man will exert influence on you; and you should not allow anyone to vouch for you, that man will loathe (?) you.

Transliterated cuneiform text
19. szu du8-a nu-e-tum3 lu2-bi sza-ba-e-dab5-be2
20. za-e szu du8-a nam-mu-e-ak-e

19. du8-a: to vouch; lu2: people;
20. za-e: you/yourself; ak: to do.

> 21: You shouldn't conduct an investigation (?) on people since the flood will return (?) the favor.

Transliterated cuneiform text
21. lu2-ra igi du8 na-an-ak-e uru2-bi sza-ri-ib-su-su

21. igi: to look/eye; uru2: flood.

> 22–27: You should not linger around a conflict; you should not allow the dispute to turn you into a witness. You should not allow (?) yourself to get involved in a disagreement. You should avoid causing a dispute;… the public plaza. Keep your distance from a dispute; you should not deviate from the path.

Transliterated cuneiform text
22. ki du14-da-ka nam-bi2-du-x-de3
23. du14-de3 lu2-ki-inim-ma nam-ba-e-ku4-ku4
24. du14-de3 ni2-zu nam-ba-[…]
25. du14 nam-ak-de3-en x […]
26. x x ka2 e2-gal-la x-am3 ba-ra-si-ga
27. du14-de3 bar-bar-ta gub-gub-ba in-nu-usz sila kur2-ra nam-ma-ni-ib-du

22. ki: place; du14: fight/conflict;
23. ki-inim-ma: place of testimony, so lu2-ki-inim-ma is a witness;
24. ni2-zu: yourself (reflexive); So du14-de3 ni2-zu is "involve yourself in a conflict". Some cuneiform symbols missing, so unclear meaning;
25. …
26. ka2 (or kan4?), unclear symbol;
27. ta: from; bar-ta: to keep away; gub: to stand; usz: distance; so "stay (at a distance) away from conflict" or "keep your distance from a conflict".

> 28–31: You must not steal anything, and you must not……yourself. You should never sneak into a household or desire for the money box (?). A thief may seem to be a lion, but once caught, he will become a slave. My son, you must not attempt thievery, and you must not hurt yourself with an axe.

Transliterated cuneiform text
28. nig2 nam-mu-zuh-zuh ni2-zu nam-mu-X-e
29. e2 na-a-an-ni-buru3-e-en mi-si-ISZ-ra al nam-me
30. ni2-zu pirig na-nam ul-dab5 sag na-nam
31. dumu-gu10 sa12 gaz nam-mu-u3-ak-e ni2-zu tun3-am3 nam-

bi2-ib-bar-re-e

28. nig2: thing; zuh: to steal; ni2-zu: yourself;
29. e2: house; buru3: to break in; mi-si-isz-ra: money box;
30. pirig: lion; na-nam: to be, so ni2-zu pririg na-nam is "yourself (i.e., the thief) is a lion", or better, considering the remaining part of the sentence, it should be "A thief might seem to be a lion..."; dab5: to catch; sag: slave; so sag na-nam becomes "to be (e.g., become) a slave";
31. dumu: composed by *dú* ('give birth') + *mú* ('to grow'), so it means 'child'; gu10: mine; dumu-gu10: my child, i.e., son; sa12 gaz: 'street robber/bandit', this word is composed by sa12: head and gaz: to crash; tun3-am3: axe.

> 32–34: You should ... a male best man...yourself(?). You should use caution while dealing with a married young lady: the defamation might be severe. You must not sit in a room with a married lady, my son.

Transliterated cuneiform text
32. nita nimgir-si na-an-ak ni2-zu na-an-X-X
33. ki-sikil dam tuku-da e-ne nam-mu-un-ne?-e inim sig-ga mah-am3
34. dumu-gu10(?) dagan-na lu2 dam tuku-da dur2 nam-bi2-e-ga2-ga2

32. nita: male; nimgir-si: paranymph/best-man; ak: to do;
33. ki-sikil: young woman; dam: wife; tuku-da: to possess; e-ne: she; un: crowd; inim: word;
sig-ga: low/weak; mah: great/severe;
34. dagan: sleeping room/chamber; dur2: to sit.

> 35–38: Do not disgrace yourself by getting into a fight with someone. You should avoid telling... falsehoods; You should not exaggerate; your statements will be taken seriously if you don't. You should avoid giving counsel for an extended period of time (?); you cannot tolerate...... stares.

Transliterated cuneiform text
35. du14 nam-mu2-mu2-de3 ni2-zu na-an-pe-el-la2
36. lul nam-guru5-guru5 sag gu2 sal-sal-la
37. ka nam-tar-tar-re-e-en inim-zu gar-ra-am3
38. ad(?) nam-gi4-gi4 igi dugud nu-mu-un-da-il2

35. pe-el-la2: equivalent to pil2, meaning disgraced/be obscure;
36. lul: lies/falsehoods; guru5: relieved of;
37. nam: na + im, meaning "certainly, truly"; ka nam-tar: to praise; inim-zu: 'words' + 'to know', so someone who knows the proper words; gar: appearance;
38. ad...gi4-gi4: to give counsel, unclear text; dugud: massive, here intented as extended.

> 39–41: You should never share stolen food with another person. You should avoid drowning your hands (?) in blood. After you have scratched the bone(?), you will be required to replace it with a sheep or ox(?).

Transliterated cuneiform text
39. lu2-zuh-a ninda zuh-a nam-mu-da-gu7-e 40. szu-zu us2-am3 na-di-ni-ib-su-su 41. giri3 hur-re gu4 sza-ba-ri-ib-su-su udu sza-ba-ri-ib-su-su
39. zuh: to steal; ninda: food; gu7: to eat;
40. szu: hand; us2: blood; su: to sink;
41. giri3: bone; hur: scratch; udu: sheep;

> 42–43: You should avoid speaking badly(?); this will eventually set you up for failure.

Transliterated cuneiform text
42. u3-nu-gar-ra na-ab-be2-a
43. egir-bi-sze3 gesz-par3-gin7 szi-me-szi-ib2-la2-e

42. u3-nu-gar-ra: fraud (pronominal prefix + "not" (nu) + "established" + nominative); na-ab-be2-a: thus does he speak;
43. eger: eventually.

44–46: You should not disperse your sheep onto unfamiliar pastures. You should never employ someone person's ox (?)(unclear)... A secure...... entails a secure trip.

Transliterated cuneiform text
44. u2 nu-kin-ga2-sze3 udu-zu sag2 nam-me
45. usz nu-se3-ga-sze3 gu4 lu2 na-hun-e
46. usz se3-ga kaskal se3-ga-am3

44. u2: pasture; kin: to send; sag2: scatter; nam-me: do not (negation).
45. gu4: bull/ox; lu2: person; hun: to hire/employ.

47: Traveling at night is dangerous because it may conceal both good and bad.

Transliterated cuneiform text
47. kaskal ge6 na-an-du sza3-bi sa6 hul-a

47. kaskal: traveler (fast travel); ge6: night; sa6: to be good; hul-a: to be bad.

48: You must not purchase a wild ass since it will only last (?) one day.

Transliterated cuneiform text
48. ansze-edin-na na-ab-sa10-sa10 u4-da-be2-esz [...]-e-zal

48. ansze-edin-na: wild ass; na: this word is used as a prohibitive prefix; sa10: to purchase; zal: this word is a measure of passing time.

49: You should avoid having sexual relations with your slave girl because she would reap you(?).

Transliterated cuneiform text
49. geme2-zu-ur2 gesz3 na-an-du3 zu ur2 szu-mu-ri-in-sa4

49. geme2: slave girl; gesz3: male penis; du3: to erect; ur2: to reap.

> 50: It's not a good idea to use harsh language while cursing since it might backfire.

Transliterated cuneiform text
50. asz2 a2 zi na-ab-bala-e szu-usz im-szi-ni10-ni10

50. asz2: to curse; a2 zi: it might reinforce the preceding noun, meaning cursing with violence; bal-a: to turn around (meaning probably 'backfire' in this context);

> 51-52: You should not pull up water that you cannot reach since it will weaken you.

Transliterated cuneiform text
51. a szu nu-gid2-i na-an-e11-de3 a2 sig szu-mu-e-ra-gal2
52. mah-bi nig2 gid2-i x ba-an-szub-be2 nig2-e ba?-an-szub-be2

51. a: water; e11: to pull up;
52. mah-bi: powerfully; nig2: thing; gid2: to pull;

> 53: If you try to dismiss a debtor, he'll turn on you.
> *1 line unclear*

Transliterated cuneiform text
53. ur5 tuku na-an-bad-e lu2-bi sza-ba-e-x-x-kur2

53. ur5: debt; tuku: creditor; bad: to move away, in the sense of 'dismiss';

> 54–57: An arrogant man will treat you like a slave girl and make your life miserable if you choose to live with him. You won't be able to go into a house without being yelled at: "There you have it! There you have it!."

Transliterated cuneiform text
54. sun7-na-da e2 na-an-da-ga2-ga2-an
55. gi4-in-sze3 du-de3 szi-me-szi-ib-szub-szub
56. ki-tusz lu2-ka na-ab-ta-bala-e-de3
57. szi-du-un szi-du-un szi-me-szi-ib2-be2-e-ne

54. sun7: arrogant; na: man; da: with, so sun7-na-da can be translated as "with an arrogant man"; ga2: house;
55. gi4-in-sze3: female slave; szub: to cast; me: to be;
56. tusz: to reside, to live with;
57. ne: with vigor; e: person; szi-me-szi-ib2-be2-e-ne: to say something with vigor/yelling

58–59: You should not remove...from the reed fence in the garden; "It must be restored! It must be restored!" They will tell you.

Transliterated cuneiform text
58. gi-sig-ga geszkiri6-ka da-ga nam-bi2-du8-e-en
59. sug6-ga-ab sug6-ga-ab szi-me-szi-ib2-be2-ne

58. gi-sig: fence; kiri6-ka: to set up, with reference to a garden;
59. sug6: to restore;

60: You should neither feed a stranger (?) nor should you settle (?) a dispute.

Transliterated cuneiform text
60. ur nam-mu-un-gu7-en du14 nam-ur3-ur3-re-en
60. ur: man; gu7: to eat; du14: fight/dispute;

61–62: My son, you must abstain from using violence (?);... You should abstain from raping someone's daughter; the neighborhood will find out.

Transliterated cuneiform text
61. dumu-mu nam-silig nam-mu-ak-en lu2 ki nam-us2-e-en
62. dumu lu2-ra gesz3 a2 zi na-an-ne-en kisal-e bi2-zu-zu

61. dumu-mu: my son; nam-silig: force/violence;
62. lu2: person; dumu lu2-ra: daughter; gesz3: penis; kisal: courtyard;

63–64: You must not attempt to drive away a strong man; you must not attempt to destroy the outer wall. You should never push a young man away; you should never turn him against the city.

Transliterated cuneiform text
63. a2-tuku na-an-bad-e-en bad3-szul-hi na-an-gul-e-en
64. gurusz na-an-bad-e-en iri-sze3 na-an-gur-re-en

63. a2-tuku: powerful/strong; bad3-szul-hi: outer wall ('city wall' + 'invader' + 'numerous'); gul: to destroy;
64. gurusz: young man;

65–66: It seems as though the slanderer's eyes are spinning around like a spindle. You should never be in his presence; his objectives (?) should not influence you.

Transliterated cuneiform text
65. lu2 inim sig-ga-ke4 igi geszbala-gin7 szi-NU-NU
66. igi-a nam-ba-e-gub-gub-bu-de3-en sza3-ge na-mu-un-kur2-kur2

65. lu2: person; inim sig-ga: slander; ke4: this symbol often occurs at the end of a genitive compound in order to make the subject as the actor of the sentence, therefore here lu2 inim sig-ga-ka4 igi can be translated as 'eyes of the slanderer'.
66. gub: to stand;

67: Breweries are not the places where you should brag like a liar, then people will believe what you say.

Transliterated cuneiform text
67. lu2-lul-la-gin7 e2 kasz-ka ka nam-tar-tar-re

67. lul: liar;

> 68–72: After becoming adult, you should refrain from leaping (?) with your hand. The warrior is unique; he is the only one who is equal to many; Utu is unique; he is the only one who is equal to many. Always put your life on the side of the warrior; always put your life on the side of Utu.

Transliterated cuneiform text
68. ki nam-nitah-ka um-me-te szu na-an-gu4-gu4-de3
69. ur-sag dili na-nam dili-ni lu2 szar2-ra-am3
70. dutu dili na-nam dili-ni lu2 szar2-ra-am3
71. ur-sag-da gub-bu-de3 zi-zu he2-en-da-gal2
72. dutu-da gub-bu-de3 zi-zu he2-en-da-gal2

68. nam-nita: manliness; szu: hand; gu4: to leap;
69. ur-sag: warrion/hero; dili: unique;
70. dutu: Utu, god of the sun;

> 73–75: Shuruppak instructed his son on these matters. Shuruppak, the son of Ubara-Tutu, instructed his son Zi-ud-sura in these matters.

Transliterated cuneiform text
73. shuruppakki-e dumu-ni-ra na sze3-mu-un-ni-in-de5
74. shuruppakki dumu ubara-tu-tu-ke4
75. zi-u4-su3-ra2 dumu-ni-ra na sze3-mu-un-ni-in-de5

> 76–82: Shuruppak instructed his son a second time. Shuruppak, the son of Ubara-Tutu, instructed his son Zi-ud-sura as follows: Allow me to offer you some advice, my son: you must pay attention! Allow me to utter a word to you, Zi-ud-sura: you must listen! Take care not to disregard my directions! Please do not violate the words I utter! An elderly man's instructions are priceless; you should follow them!

Transliterated cuneiform text
76. 2(disz)-kam-ma-sze3 szuruppakki-e dumu-ni-ra na-mu-un-de5-de5
77. szuruppakki dumu ubara-tu-tu-ke4
78. zi-u4-su3-ra2 dumu-ni-ra na na-mu-un-de5-de5

79. dumu-mu na ga-de5 na-de5-mu he2-dab5
80. zi-u4-su3-ra2 inim ga-ra-ab-du11 gizzal he2-em-szi-ak
81. na-de5-ga-mu szu nam-bi2-bar-re-en
82. inim du11-ga-ga2 na-ab-ta-bala-e-de3-en
82a. na-de5 ab-ba nig2 kal-la-am3 gu2-zu he2-e

83–91: The lips of a beer drinker... My youngest one... The lips of a beer drinker... Ninkasi... *5 lines unclear*

Transliterated cuneiform text
83. ka kasz nag-a [...] x-kam
84. lu2-tur-mu [...] lu2 x [...]
85. ka kasz nag-a [...] x
86. dnin-ka-si [...]
87. [...] KA x ur3 he2-x IM
88. [...]-ur3-ur3-re
89. [...] x a mu-un-ni-ib2-il2-il2
90. [...] x im-sar-re
91. KA x sag im-ta-ab-gur4-gur4-re

92–93: It's not going to be repaid by your own man. Slander may be hidden (?) among the reeds since they are...

Transliterated cuneiform text
92. lu2 ni2-za-ke4 nu-e-szi-su-su
93. gesz-gi masz2 u2 na-nam sza3-bi inim sig-ga-am3

94–96: The palace is like a potent river: in the middle is like goring bulls, there is never enough water to fill it, and there is no way to stop it from flowing.

Transliterated cuneiform text
94. e2-gal i7 mah-am3 sza3-bi gu4 du7-du7-dam
95. nig2 ku4-ku4 nig2 sa2 nu-di-dam
96. nig2 e3 nig2 nu-silig-ge-dam

97–100: It is simple to say "I will gift it to you" when it comes to someone else's bread, but the moment of real offering might be as distant as the sky. If you pursue the person who said, "I will give it to you," he will answer, "I cannot offer it to you since the bread has now been consumed."

Transliterated cuneiform text
97. ninda lu2-ka ga-ra-ab-szum2-bi ku-nu-a
98. szum2-mu-da-bi an ba9-ra2-am3
99. ga-ra-ab-szum2-bi lu2-ra ga-ni-in-us2
100. nu-ra-ab-szum2-mu ninda igi-bi-sze3 til-la-am3

101–102: Property is something that can be increased (?), but nothing can compare to my children.

Transliterated cuneiform text
101. nig2-u2-rum nig2 a2 se3-ga-a-da
102. lu2-tur-mu nig2 nu-mu-un-da-sa2

103–105: The poetic mouth utters poetry; the stern mouth delivers legal documents; and the gentle mouth collects herbs for pleasant tea.

Transliterated cuneiform text
103. ka sa6-sa6-ge inim i3-szid-e
104. ka du3-du3-e kiszib3 i3-il2-il2
105. ka lal3-e u2-lal3 e-bur12-re

106–108: The liar delivers a full sack of bread; the arrogant brings an empty bag and can only fill his empty mouth with bragging.

Transliterated cuneiform text
106. ka tuku kuszlu-ub2-a-ni sa2 im-du11
107. gal-gal di kuszlu-ub2 sug4-ga sza-mu-un-de6
108. silim du11 ka sug4-ga sza-ba-ni-ib-gar

109: Anyone who deals with leather eventually (?) has to work with leather that they have made themselves.

Transliterated cuneiform text
109. kusz du3-du3-e kusz-ni sze3-ba-e-du3-e

110: Anyone's hand can't hold the strong one.

Transliterated cuneiform text
110. usu-tuku szu lu2-ta sza-ba-ra-an-tum3

111-114: In the end, the foolish pays the price. The foolish loses something while asleep. "Let me go, please!", he screams, as though begging for his life.

Transliterated cuneiform text
111. lu2lil-e nig2 u2-gu i3-ib-de2-e
112. u3?-sa2 lu2lil-e nig2 u2-gu i3-de2-e
113. na-an-kesz2-kesz2-re-de3 giri17 szu am3-mi-in-gal2
114. ga-ti-la giri17 szu am3-mi-in-gal2

115–117: Fate is decreed by the reckless. The shameless heaps (?) things on someone else's shoulders, saying, "I am such that I deserve adoration."

Transliterated cuneiform text
115. sag-du nu-tuku nam szi-ib-tar-re
116. tesz2 nu-tuku lu2 ur2-sze3 mu-un-de2-e
117. ge26-e na-nam u6-e ba-gub

118: A feeble woman is always possessed (?) by destiny.

Transliterated cuneiform text
118. dam dim3-e nam? tar-re ba-dab5-dab5

119–123: A worker that you employ will share the bread bag with you; he will eat with you from the same bag, and he will complete the bag with you if you hire him. Then he will stop working with you and, claiming that "I have to survive on something," he would go to the palace and serve there.

Transliterated cuneiform text

119. lu2 hun-ga2-zu kuszlu-ub2 szi-me-da-ba-e
120. kuszlu-ub2 szi-ma-da-gu7-e
121. kuszlu-ub2 szi-me-da-til-e
122. ga2-la szi-me-da-dag-ge
123. ga-ba-ra-gu7 e2-gal-la ba-gub

124–125: You summon your son to your residence; you summon your daughter to her women's chambers.
Transliterated cuneiform text
124. dumu-nita-zu e2-zu-sze3 im-me
125. dumu-munus-zu ama5-ni-sze3 im-me

126: When you consume beer, you should refrain from passing judgment.
Transliterated cuneiform text
126. kasz nag-a-zu-ne di na-an-ne-e

127: You should not worry unduly about what leaves the house.
Transliterated cuneiform text
127. e2-ta e3 sza3-zu na-an-gu7-e

128–130: Although heaven is farthest and earth is most valuable, it is via heaven that you increase your possessions and all distant nations breathe.
Transliterated cuneiform text
128. an su3-u4-dam ki kal-kal-la-am3
129. an-da nig2 im-da-lu-lu-un
130. kur-kur-re zi szi-im-da-pa-an-pa

131–133: It is proper, my son, that during harvest, the most valuable period of the year, you should gather like a slave girl and dine like a queen.
Transliterated cuneiform text
131. u4 buru14-sze3 u4 kal-kal-la-sze3
132. geme2-gin7 de5-ga-ab egir2-gin7 gu7-a

133. dumu-mu geme2-gin7 ri egir2-gin7 gu7-a ur5 he2-en-na-nam-ma-am3

134–142: Whoever insults has the potential to harm just the skin; voracious eyes (?) on the other hand, have the potential to murder. The liar, yelling, rips his clothes to shreds. Insults serve as (?) counsel to the wicked. Arrogance is like to an abscess: a stomach-turning weed. Abundance comes through my prayers. Prayer is a refreshing drink that soothes the soul. The people of the Land are only interested in (?) insults and stupidity.

Transliterated cuneiform text
134. asz2 du11-du11-ge bar szi-in-dar
135. igi-tum3 la2 sag gesz im-ra-ra
136. gu3 mur-re lu2-lul-e tug2 szi-bir7-bir7-e
137. asz2 di nig2-erim2-e na-de5 sze3-il2-il2
138. inim dirig u3-bu-bu-ul-la-am3 u2 lipisz gig-ga-am3
139. MU dar-dar-da ga-mu-e-da-zalag-ge
140. inim szudu3-de3-mu he2-gal2-la-am3
141. a-ra-zu a sedx(KAD3)-da sza3-ge im-sedx(KAD3)-e
142. asz2 di? na-ga2-ah di-da gizzal kalam-ma-ke4

143–145: Shuruppak instructed his son on these matters. Shuruppak, the son of Ubara-Tutu, instructed his son Zi-ud-sura in these matters.

Transliterated cuneiform text
143. szuruppakki-e dumu-ni-ra na sze3-mu-ni-in-de5
144. szuruppakki dumu ubara-tu-tu-ke4
145. zi-u4-su3-ra2 dumu-ni-ra na sze-mu-ni-in-de5

146–152: Shuruppak instructed his son a third time. Zi-ud-sura, the son of Shuruppak, the son of Ubara-Tutu, was given these instructions by his father: Please, my son, listen to what I have to say. Here's a word for you, Zi-ud-sura: pay attention! Don't forget what I told you! Please don't go against what I say! (*addition 152a*: It's important to follow an elderly man's advice, even if you don't agree with it!)

Transliterated cuneiform text
146. 3(disz)-kam-ma-sze3 szuruppakki dumu-ni-ra na na-mu-un-de5-de5
147. szuruppakki dumu ubara-tu-tu-ke4
148. zi-u4-su3-ra na sze3-mu-ni-in-de5
149. dumu-mu na ga-de5 na-de5-mu he2-dab5
150. zi-u4-su3-ra2 inim ga-ra-ab-du11 gizzal he2-em-szi-ak
151. na-de5-ga-mu nam-bi2-bar-re
152. inim du11-ga-mu na-ab-ta-bala-e-de3
152a. na-de5 ab-ba nig2 kal-la-am3 gu2-zu he2-em-szi-ak

> 153: You must not retaliate against the son of a peasant farmer: he built (?) your dykes and canals.

Transliterated cuneiform text
dumu engar-ra-ra nigz2 nam-mu-ra-ra-an eg2 pa5-zu sze3-em-ra

> 154–164: You must not purchase a prostitute because she has a biting mouth. You should not purchase a house-born slave: he is a stomach-turning weed. You should never purchase a free individual because he will constantly rest against the wall. You should avoid purchasing a royal slave girl since she will always be at the bottom of the barrel (?). You must bring down a foreign slave from the highlands, or someone from a region where he is a foreigner; my son, then he will pour water for you where the sun rises, and he will walk alongside of you. He doesn't have any family, so he doesn't want to visit them; he doesn't have any city, so he doesn't want to visit his city. He is not permitted to knock on the door of..., nor is he permitted to enter... He will not... with you, and he will not be arrogant with you.

Transliterated cuneiform text
154. kar-ke4 na-an-sa10-sa10-an ka u4-sar-ra-kam
155. ama-a-tu na-an-sa10-sa10-an u2 lipisz gig-ga-am3
156. dumu-gi7 na-an-sa10-sa10-an za3 e2-gar8-e us2-sa-am3

157. geme2 e2-gal-la na-an-sa10-sa10-an giri3 dur2-bi-sze3 gal2-gal2-la-am3
158. sag kur-ra kur-bi-ta um-ta-a-e11
159. lu2 ki nu-zu-a-ni-ta u3-mu-e-de6
160. dumu-mu ki dutu e3-a-asz
161. a hu-mu-ra-an-de2-e igi-zu-sze3 he2-du
162. e2 nu-tuku e2-a-ni-sze3 la-ba-du
163. iri nu-tuku iri-ni-sze3 la-ba-du
163a. geszig x [...] szu la?-ba-an-da-us2-sa
163b. x x x-sze3 la-ba-an-da-ku4-ku4
164. la-ba-e-da-hi-li-e la-ba-e-da-sun7-e

165–167: My son, please don't go east on your own. Your friend should not have...

Transliterated cuneiform text
165. dumu-mu ki dutu e3-a-asz
166. dili-zu-ne kaskal na-an-ni-du-un
167. lu2 zu-a-zu sag szu UD ba-ra-ak-ke4

168–169: A name superimposed over another......; you should not build a mountain on top of another.

Transliterated cuneiform text
168. mu mu-a se3-ga sag-du lu2-u3-ra im-ma?-x-e
169. kur-ra kur na-an-na-dub-be2

170–171: When it comes to fate, it's like a damp bank that might make you fall.

Transliterated cuneiform text
170. nam-tar pesz10 dur5-ra-am3
171. lu2-da giri3-ni im-ma-da-an-ze2-er

172–174: It's true that the older brother acts as a father figure, and the older sister as a mother figure. Respect your older brother and treat your elder sister with the deference due a parent.

Transliterated cuneiform text

172. szesz-gal a-a na-nam nin9 gal ama na-nam
173. szesz-gal-zu-ur2 gizzal he2-em-szi-ak
174. nin9 gal ama-zu-gin7 gu2 he2-em-szi-gal2

175–176: Working alone with your eyes is a pointless exercise, and neither is multiplying your goods solely with your words.

Transliterated cuneiform text
175. za-e igi-zu-ta kin na-an-ak-e
176. ka-zu-ta nig2-nam nu-lu-lu-un

177: The careless one destroys (?) his family.

Transliterated cuneiform text
177. ga2-la dag-ge e2 dur2-bi-sze3 mu-un-gen

178–180: In the same way that hunger drives some people to the mountains, it also attracts traitors and outsiders, who must be fed to survive.

Transliterated cuneiform text
178. ninda-e lu2 kur-ra bi2-in-e11-de3
179. lu2-lul lu2 bar-ra bi2-in-tum2-mu
180. ninda-e lu2 kur-ta im-ma-da-ra-an-e11-de3

181–182: A tiny town gives its monarch a calf, whereas a big city digs a home site for him (?).

Transliterated cuneiform text
181. uru2 tur-re lugal-bi-ir amar szi-in-ga-an-u3-tu
182. uru2 mah-e e2 du3-a szi-hur-re

183–188: ... is really well-equipped. The poor guy infects the affluent man with a variety of diseases. The married guy is well-equipped; the single man must make his bed in a haystack (?). Whoever intends to demolish a home will do so; whoever wishes to elevate it will do so.

Transliterated cuneiform text
183. [...] x-ke4 a2 szu im-du7-du7

184. lu2 nig2-tuku lu2 nig2 nu-tuku gig sze3-em-gar
185. lu2 dam tuku a2 szu im-du7-du7
186. dam nu-un-tuku sze-er-tab-ba mu-un-nu2
187. e2 gul-gul-lu-de3 e2 sza-ba-da-an-gul-e
188. lu2 zi-zi-i-de3 lu2 sza-ba-da-an-zi-zi-i

189–192: You may cross the river by grabbing the neck of a massive ox. My son, if you follow in the footsteps of your city's great leaders, you will undoubtedly rise to prominence.

Transliterated cuneiform text
189. gu4 mah-a gu2-bi lu2 a-ba-an-dab5
190. lu2 i7-da ba-ra-an-bala-e
191. lu2 gu-la iri-za-ka za3-ba u3-ba-e-zal-ta
192. dumu-mu za-a ur5-re he2-em-me-re-a-e11-de3

193–201: Bringing a slave girl from the mountains into your life has the potential to bring about both positive and bad outcomes. The hands hold the good; the heart holds the bad. Neither the good nor the bad can be released from the heart's grasp. Because of this, the heart never gives up on what is good. If you're looking for evil, you've found it…..
(*There are at least two lines of text that are ambiguous in this passage, 199a & 199b.*) May the evil-boat doer's drown in the river! May his waterskin crack in the sands of the desert!

Transliterated cuneiform text
193. geme2-zu hur?-sag-ta szi-im-ta-an-tum3 sa6 szi-im-ta-an-de6
194. hul szi-in-ga-am3-ta-an-tum3
195. sa6-ga szu-am3 hul sza3 an-ga-am3
196. sa6-ga sza3-ge szu nu-bar-re
197. hul sza3-ge szu nu-di-ni-bar-re
198. sa6-ga ki dur5-ru-am3 sza3-ge nu-da13-da13
199. hul e2 nig2-gur11-ra ur5-e la-ba-an-gu7-e
199a. mu-un-sa6 mu-un-sa6
199b. ka-ni mu-un-tag-tag
200. hul-da i7-da ma2? he2-en-da-su

201. an-edin-na kuszummu he2-en-da-dar

202–203: Loving people keep their families together, while cruel people break them apart.

Transliterated cuneiform text
202. sza3 ki ag2 nig2 e2 du3-du3-u3-dam
203. sza3 hul gig nig2 e2 gul-gul-lu-dam

204–207: Princely divine abilities include the ability to rule, to amass wealth, and to remain steady. Be obedient to those who are respected and humble yourself before those who are strong. When you do this, my son, you'll be able to stand up (?) to the evildoers.

Transliterated cuneiform text
204. nir-gal2-e nig2-tuku gaba-gal2 me nam-nun-na
205. nir-gal2-ra gu2 he2-en-ne-ni-gal2
206. a2-tuku ni2-zu he2-en-ne-szi-la2
207. dumu-mu lu2 hul-gal2-ra he2-en-ne-szi-gal2-le

208–212: You should avoid marrying at a festivity. Her inside is deceptive (?), as is her exterior. Her silver is borrowed, as is her lapis lazuli. Her outfit is borrowed, as is the linen robe she is wearing. Nothing (?) comes close to...

Transliterated cuneiform text
208. ezem-ma-ka dam na-an-tuku-tuku-e
209. sza3-ga hun-ga2-am3 bar-ra hun-ga2-am3
210. ku3 hun-ga2-am3 za-gin3 hun-ga2-am3
211. tug2? hun-ga2-am3 gada? hun-ga2-am3
212. [...] nu-mu-un-da-sa2

213–214: You should not purchase a.... bull. You should not purchase a ferocious bull;...a gap (?) in the corral...

Transliterated cuneiform text
213. gu4 [...] na-an-ni-sa10-sa10
214. gu4 lul-la na-sa10-sa10 e2 tur3 buru3 x x [...]

215: One selects (?) a trustworthy wife to maintain a nice home.

Transliterated cuneiform text
215. munus zi e2 zi-sze3 lu2 szi-in-gar

216–217: Buy a donkey at a different time. You should not buy one during harvest. A donkey that eats... will eat with another donkey.

Transliterated cuneiform text
216. u4 buru14-ka ansze na-an-sa10-sa10
217. ansze la gu7 ansze-da im-[...]

218–219: A donkey that is mean hangs its neck. However, a mean man, my son,...

Transliterated cuneiform text
218. ansze lul-la gu2-tar im-la2
219. dumu-mu lu2-lul-e za3-si mu-un-sa6-sa6

220: A woman who owns her own home wrecks the house.

Transliterated cuneiform text
220. munus bar-szu-gal2-e e2 dur2-bi-sze3 mu-un-gen

221: Drinking too much may ruin the crop.

Transliterated cuneiform text
221. kurun nag-nag-e buru14 im-su-su-su

222–234: A woman intruder (?) ... a ladder and flies into the homes like a fly. A female donkey... on the street. A sow feeds its young on the street. A woman who pierced herself starts to cry and holds the spindle that pierced her in her hand. She goes into every house and looks at every street. She says, "Get out!" over and over. She looks around (?) from all the rooftops. She sneezes where there is a fight.
2 lines aren't clear

Instructions of Shuruppak: Commentary 37

Transliterated cuneiform text
222. salszu-ku6 geszkun5 lu2 2(disz)-e da nu-DI
223. e2-a nim-gin7 mi-ni-ib-dal-dal-en
224. eme3 sila-a inim i3-szid-e
225. |SAL.SZUL| sila-a dumu-ni-ra ga mu-ni-ib-gu7-e
226. munus giri17 hur ak szeg11 gi4-gi4-dam
227. geszbala hur-ra szu-na na-mu-un-gal2
228. e2-e2-a i-in-ku4-ku4-ku4
229. e-sir2-e-sir2-ra gu2 mu-un-gi-gi-de3
230. da ur3-ra im-me im-me e3-ab
231. bad3-si-bad3-si-a igi mu-szi-x-il2-il2?-e
232. ki du14-de3 gal2-la-sze3 zi im-x-pa?-pa-an-e?
233. ki mu-szub-ba a2-za x x x IM x
234. zi x gi4 ESZ mu-un-ne?-pa3 im-mi-ni-du11

Love (?) someone who doesn't love (?). My son,...
several unclear lines
A heart that is filled with happiness.

Transliterated cuneiform text
235. x x-ke4 sza3 hul gig tuku-tuku
236. dumu-mu [...] gum2-gamx(LUM) mi-ni-ib-za
237. [...] A x x IN TAR
238. [...] x x [...] tum3
239. [...] nu2
240. [...] DU
241. sza3 hul2-la i-im-dirig-ge [...]

242–244: Nothing should be treasured, but life should be enjoyable. Things should serve you, not the other way around. My son,...

Transliterated cuneiform text
242. nig2-nam nu-kal zi ku7-ku7-da
243. nig2 nam-kal-kal-en nig2-e me-kal-kal
244. dumu-mu gun3-gun3-gin7 igi gun3-gun3

245: You should not ...... grain; its ...... are numerous.

Transliterated cuneiform text
245. dezina2-ra na-an-kesz2-kesz2-re-de3-en gesza2-bi i3-szar2

246–247: If you mistreat a sheep, she will bear you a daughter. In order to avoid giving birth to a son, do not place a lump of soil in the money chest(?).

Transliterated cuneiform text
246. kir11-e asz2 nam-en dumu-munus in-u3-tu-un
247. geszmi-si-ISZ-a lag nam-bi2-szub-be2-en dumu-nita in-u3-tu-un

248–249: You should not kidnap a woman and make her weep (?). The location where the woman is kidnapped...

Transliterated cuneiform text
248. dam nam-mu-un-kar-re-en gu3 KA na-an-ga2-ga2
249. ki dam kar-re nam-silig gum-ga2-am3

250–251: Let us go in circles (?) while saying, "Oh, my foot, oh, my neck!" Let us construct a tremendous bow with unified forces (?)!

Transliterated cuneiform text
250. a giri3 a gu2 nigin2-na ga-am3-me-re7-de3-en
251. lu2 gu-la a2 1(disz)-e ga-na-gam-me-en-de3

252–253: You must not murder a...... since he is a kid conceived by...... You should not murder ...in the manner of...; you should not tie him.

Transliterated cuneiform text
252. galam-ma na-an-ug5-ge-en dumu in-sug4-ge tu-da
253. en-ra BAD-a-gin7 dnanna-ug5-ge-en szu na-an-du3-du3-en

254: The destiny of their master is decided by the wet-nurses in the women's chambers.

Transliterated cuneiform text
254. emeda-ga-la2 ama5-a-ke4 lugal-bi-ir nam szi-im-mi-ib-tar-

re

255-260: You should not be rude to your mother, because that makes her hate you. Mother and God are two people who you should not question. Mother, like Utu, gives birth to the man, and the father, like a deity, makes him powerful (?). The father is like a deity, and his words are trustworthy. It is necessary to follow the father's directions.

Transliterated cuneiform text
255. ama-zu-ur2 inim dirig nam-ba-na-ab-be2-en hul sza-ba-ra-gig-ga-am3
256. inim ama-za inim dingir-za ka-sze3 nam-bi2-ib-dib2-be2-en
257. ama dutu-am3 lu2 mu-un-u3-tu
258. ab-ba dingir-ra-am3 x mu-un-dadag-ge
259. ab-ba dingir-am3 inim-ma-ni zi-da
260. na-de5 ab-ba-sze3 gizzal he2-em-szi-ia-ak

261: A city would also be devoid of a center if it lacked periphery.

Transliterated cuneiform text
261. e2 iri bar-ra-ke4 iri sza3-ga szi-du3-du3-e

262–263: My son, no matter how damp or dry it is, the field at the foot of the dikes provides a source of revenue.

Transliterated cuneiform text
262. dumu-mu GAN2 e dur2-bi-sze3 gal2-la
263. al-duru5 szukur2-ra-am3 al-had2 szukur2-ra-am3

264: It seems incomprehensible (?) that anything could be lost in perpetuity.

Transliterated cuneiform text
264. nig2 u2-gu de2-a nig2-me-gar-ra

265: ...of Dilmum, the place where the sun rises...

Transliterated cuneiform text
265. uruda?gin2 dilmunki-na sa10-sze3 TE-ga

> 266-271: Getting lost is unpleasant for a dog, but dreadful for a man. On the strange path along the mountains' edge, the gods of the mountains are man-eaters. They do not construct homes in the same way that men do; they do not construct towns in the same way that men do.
> 1 line is ambiguous
> *1 line unclear*

Transliterated cuneiform text
266a. ur nu-zu hul-am3 lu2 nu-zu husz-am3
266b. ki nu-zu husz-am3 ur nu-zu tesz2-am3
267. kaskal nu-zu gaba kur-ra-ka
268. dingir kur-ra lu2 gu7-gu7-u3-me-esz
269. e2 lu2-gin7 nu-du3 iri lu2-gin7 nu-du3
270. ki-zu-a lu2-ka lu2 sza-ba-ra-an-e3-de3
271. sipa-ra kin-kin mu-na-til udu gi4-gi4 mu-na-til

> 272-273: The shepherd had given up looking for the sheep and had ceased bringing them back. He stopped plowing the land for the farmer (?).
> *1 line unclear*

Transliterated cuneiform text
272. engar-ra a-sza3 ur11-ru mu-na-til
273a. ... x gi4 mu-na-KU-en?
273b. ... la ... u2 de5-ge ...

> 274-276: In the castle, the mind is soothed by this gift of words... Stars are a gift... of many words.

Transliterated cuneiform text
274. kadra inim-ma-bi nig2 sza3 ten-na mu?-[...]
275. e2-gal-la ku4-ra-bi nig2 sza3 ten-na [...]
276. kadra inim-inim-ma mul [...]

> 277: Ubara Tutu's son, Shuruppak, gave his instructions in the form of these rules.

Transliterated cuneiform text
277. na-de5 szuruppakki dumu ubara-tu-tu-ke4 na-de5-ga

> 278–280: Praise be to the maiden Nisaba, who finished the great tablets and received instructions from Shuruppak, the son of Ubara-Tutu.

Transliterated cuneiform text
278. szuruppakki dumu ubara-tu-tu-ke4 na-de5-ga
279. nin dub gal-gal-la szu du7-a
280. ki-sikil dnisaba za3-mi2

Printed in Great Britain
by Amazon